Myraki Publishing 2018

Mother of the Bride
Shit To Do
Journal

Made in the USA
Middletown, DE
15 December 2019

80798795R00046